8 FACTS ABOUT THE WILD MAN.

By

Dr TIMOTHY KESSINGTON.

copyright © (DR TIMOTHY KESSINGTON, Ph.D., PsyD) 2023. All rights reserved

Before this document is duplicated or reproduced in any manner, the publisher's consent must be gained.

Therefore, the contents within can neither be stored electronically, transferred, nor kept in a database. Neither in part nor in full can the document be copied, scanned, faxed, or retained without approval from the publisher or creator.

TABLE OF CONTENTS

ABOUT THE AUTHOR

Dr. TIMOTHY KESSINGTON is a licensed psychologist in the state of texas. he is a certified counselor on marriage and relationship/mental health. He is passionate to the core to see people in relationships happy and couples achieve the best out of every relationship.

INTRODUCTION:

"The Out of Control Man: An Extensive Investigation"
In the records of mankind's set of experiences and folklore, the idea of the Crazy Man has endured as a dazzling and mysterious figure. The out-of-control Man, frequently portrayed as a basic, untamed being inhabiting the edges of society, has tracked down its direction into the social stories of various civic establishments. This complete investigation looks to take apart the diverse ideas of the out-of-control Man, jumping profoundly into its authentic roots, social appearances, mental translations, and contemporary significance. Through eight unmistakable sections, we set out on an excursion to

disentangle the intricacies encompassing this fascinating original.

CHAPTER 1: BEGINNINGS AND ADVANCEMENT.

Beginnings and Development" regularly alludes to the early part of a book or record where the central perspectives, verifiable foundation, or starting phases of a subject, point, or story are investigated and made sense of, frequently making way for what continues in resulting sections

CHAPTER 2 : SOCIAL POINTS OF VIEW.

Social Viewpoints investigates the unpredictable woven artwork of human social orders, digging into how assorted traditions, dialects, and customs shape our reality. For example, the festival of Diwali in India with its dynamic lights and merry soul stands out from the gravity of a Japanese tea service, exhibiting the rich social varieties that characterize our worldwide scene

CHAPTER 3: MENTAL ASPECTS.

Mental Aspects digs into the complex features of the human psyche, investigating subjects like perception, feeling, and conduct. It inspects how mental cycles like memory and critical thinking shape how we might interpret the world, how feelings impact independent direction, and how mental elements support our reactions to stress and injury. Through illustrative examinations, it discloses the intricacy of the human way of behaving, revealing insight into the interaction between science, climate, and individual experience, at last giving significant bits of knowledge into the confounding domain of human brain research.

CHAPTER 4: WRITING AND CRAFTSMANSHIP.

Writing and Workmanship investigate the complex exchange of imagination and culture, digging into how craftsmanship and composed articulation have generally reflected cultural movements. For example, during the Renaissance, the assembly of visual workmanship and writing in works like Leonardo da Vinci's journals exemplified how these types of articulation can commonly motivate and enhance each other, moulding the course of mankind's set of experiences and scholarly turn of events.

CHAPTER 5: FABLES AND FANTASIES.

Fables and Fantasies dive into the rich woven artwork of humans narrating, investigating the social stories and legends that went down through the ages. Envision a pit fire, where seniors recap old stories, passing on the insight and upsides of their general public to excited youthful personalities. Fables include a horde of stories, from the Greek legends of divine beings and legends like Zeus and Hercules to the legendary adventures of Norse folklore, highlighting Odin and Thor. These accounts, frequently interlaced with history, shape how we might interpret the world, our beginnings, and our ethical compass. The section takes apart these deep-rooted accounts, looking at their part in moulding societies and the persevering power they hold in our aggregate creative minds. It welcomes perusers to look into the profundities of human imagination and conviction, where legends and fantasies proceed to charm and motivate across time and boundaries.

CHAPTER 6: THE ADVANCE OUT OF CONTROL MAN.

The Cutting edge Crazy Man digs into the advancement of manliness and the changing cultural assumptions put on men in the 21st 100 years. This part investigates how conventional ideas of manliness, represented by the rough outdoorsman, have given way to a more nuanced and different comprehension of being a man today.

Delineation 1: The Change in Jobs The section examines how the cutting edge out of control man no longer sticks stringently to the conventional jobs of supplier and defender. All things considered, men are urged to embrace a more extensive scope of jobs, from supporting parental figures to sincerely expressive m accomplices.

: representation 2, The ability to appreciate anyone on a deeper level: The idea of the cutting-edge crazy man features the significance of the capacity to understand individuals at their core and mindfulness. Men are urged to investigate their sentiments, look for help when required, and focus on psychological wellness.

Representation 3: Breaking Generalizations - The part features genuine instances of men who challenge orientation generalizations by chasing after vocations in fields customarily overwhelmed by ladies, like nursing or remaining at-home nurturing.

Outline 4: Diversity - The underscores the diversity of manliness, recognizing that the experience of being a cutting-edge crazy man can fluctuate essentially based on factors like race, sexuality, and financial status.

CHAPTER 7: ORIENTATION AND CHARACTER.

Orientation and Personality investigate the complicated connection between orientation and one's healthy self-appreciation, digging into the complex manners by which people see and express their character according to their orientation. This examines the cultural builds and assumptions related to orientation jobs, featuring how these standards can impact a singular's self-idea. Through powerful private stories and humanistic examination, it explains the nuanced encounters of individuals exploring their orientation personalities, at last, revealing insight into the significance of understanding and regarding different articulations of self in the present progressively comprehensive society.

CHAPTER 8: THE CRAZY MAN IN THE COMPUTERIZED AGE.

.

The Out of Control Man in the Computerized Age" investigates the idea of the "Crazy Man" as a representation of the untamed, basic parts of human instinct that arise about our undeniably digitized and mechanically determined world. In this section, the creator dives into how, amidst the quick progressions in innovation, we wrestle with basic inquiries regarding our personality, our relationship with nature, and our position in the advanced scene. The Crazy Man addresses the untamed substance of humankind that opposes similarity and difficulties with the limits of our controlled, advanced presence. Through striking stories and interesting models, this part urges perusers to consider persevering through a battle between our basic senses and the computerized facade of present-day life.

CONCLUSION:

All in all, our far-reaching investigation of the Crazy Man model has uncovered its perseverance through interest and flexibility all through mankind's set of experiences. From its old beginnings to its contemporary indications, the Crazy Man keeps on dazzling our creative mind and offers significant bits of knowledge into our social, mental, and social scenes. As we close this examination, we perceive that the Crazy Man's puzzling presence in our shared mindset welcomes progressing investigation, reflection, and reevaluation.

www.ingramcontent.com/pod-product-compliance
Lightning Source LLC
Chambersburg PA
CBHW060912260726
48661CB00008B/3592